HARRIERS

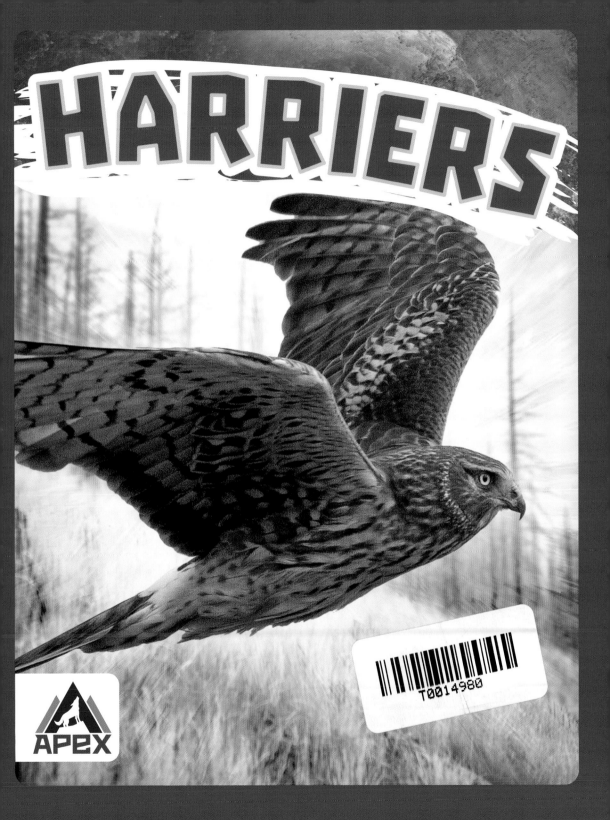

APEX

BY CONNOR STRATTON

WWW.APEXEDITIONS.COM

Apex is distributed by North Star Editions:
sales@northstareditions.com | 888-417-0195

Produced for Apex by Red Line Editorial.

Photographs ©: Shutterstock Images, cover (bird), 1 (bird), 4–5, 6–7, 8–9, 10–11, 12, 13, 14–15, 16–17, 18–19, 20–21, 21, 22–23, 24, 25, 26–27, 29; Unsplash, cover (background), 1 (background)

Library of Congress Control Number: 2021915667

ISBN
978-1-63738-143-4 (hardcover)
978-1-63738-179-3 (paperback)
978-1-63738-250-9 (ebook pdf)
978-1-63738-215-8 (hosted ebook)

Printed in the United States of America
Mankato, MN
012022

NOTE TO PARENTS AND EDUCATORS

Apex books are designed to build literacy skills in striving readers. Exciting, high-interest content attracts and holds readers' attention. The text is carefully leveled to allow students to achieve success quickly. Additional features, such as bolded glossary words for difficult terms, help build comprehension.

TABLE OF CONTENTS

CHAPTER 1

FLYING LOW

A northern harrier flies over a field. The bird is hunting for **prey**. It flies just above the thick grass.

Harriers often fly very close to the ground when they hunt.

Male northern harriers have gray feathers. Females are brown. Most females are larger, too.

The harrier listens carefully. It hears a faint sound. A mouse is running along the ground.

GRAY GHOSTS

Male northern harriers are often called "gray ghosts." They get this name because of how they hunt. The birds **hover** quietly in the air. Their gray feathers look ghostly.

The harrier pounces. It grabs the mouse with its sharp claws. Then the bird lands to eat. The mouse will make a good meal.

Most birds of prey hunt by sight. But harriers use both hearing and sight.

Harriers use their sharp beaks to tear their food.

CHAPTER 2

LIFE IN THE WILD

Harriers can be found throughout most of the world. They often live in open areas. Many make their homes in fields. Others live in **marshes**.

Western marsh harriers live in many countries throughout Africa, Asia, and Europe.

Harriers often make nests in tall grass or reeds.

Harriers make nests on the ground. They tend to **breed** in areas where many plants grow. That way, their nests are hidden from **predators**.

Harriers usually have four or five babies at a time.

Baby harriers stay in the nest for a few weeks after they hatch from eggs.

Many harriers **migrate** south during winter. But some stay in the same area all year.

Many pallid harriers migrate from Europe to Africa for the winter. They fly back to Europe in the spring.

HARRIERS ON FARMS

People have cleared many wild areas to make farms. As a result, many harriers lost their homes. Some harriers stayed on the farms. But farmers sometimes destroyed their nests by accident.

There are about a dozen different types of harriers.

CHAPTER 3

LONG TAILS, LONG WINGS

Harriers can grow to be 20 inches (51 cm) long. They have long tails. Their tails help them turn quickly as they fly.

Marsh harriers are the largest type of harriers. Their wings can spread more than 50 inches (127 cm).

Harriers don't depend on speed to hunt. Instead, they fly over land and swoop down to catch prey.

Harriers have long, wide wings. They don't need to flap as much as other large birds. As a result, they can fly more slowly. Harriers can fly quietly, too.

Some harriers have sideways stripes called bars on their feathers.

Harriers can be brown or black. They can also be gray or white. Males often have different colors or markings than females.

Male pied harriers have grayish-white and black feathers.

Young pied harriers are golden. Females grow up to have brown and white feathers.

CHANGING COLORS

Young harriers can be different colors than adults. For example, young northern harriers have bright-orange bellies. The feathers change colors as the birds grow up.

CHAPTER 4

HOW HARRIERS HUNT

Harriers eat many kinds of small animals. They often hunt **rodents**. Some also eat snakes, frogs, and birds.

Harriers often eat rats or mice. They may also catch rabbits or ducks.

Harriers catch prey with their feet.

Harriers usually hunt during the day. They search for prey. They fly back and forth over fields.

HUNTING THE HUNTERS

Grouse are wild birds that live on the ground. Many people hunt them. Hen harriers eat grouse. So, people sometimes hunt the harriers. They try to stop the harriers from killing the grouse.

Hen harriers live in the United Kingdom. They are at risk of dying out.

A harrier's face has **stiff** feathers. These feathers are shaped in a circle. Sounds hit the feathers. The feathers guide the sounds to the bird's ears. Harriers can find prey this way.

A bird's ears are small openings on the sides of its head. Feathers cover them up.

A harrier's feathers make its face look similar to an owl's.

COMPREHENSION QUESTIONS

Write your answers on a separate piece of paper.

1. Write a sentence describing how harriers hunt their prey.

2. Harriers often eat rodents. What is your favorite food to eat? Why do you like it?

3. Where do a harrier's stiff feathers guide sound toward?

    A. toward the bird's ears

    B. toward the bird's eyes

    C. toward the bird's feet

4. How does building nests among plants help harriers hide from predators?

    A. No predators live in areas with thick plants.

    B. Predators cannot find the nests as easily.

    C. Predators will eat the plants instead.

5. What does **faint** mean in this book?

*The harrier listens carefully. It hears a **faint** sound. A mouse is running along the ground.*

    A. big and loud

    B. small or quiet

    C. falling apart

6. What does **pounces** mean in this book?

*The harrier **pounces**. It grabs the mouse with its sharp claws.*

    A. moves high up into the air

    B. moves slowly to run away

    C. moves quickly to catch prey

Answer key on page 32.

GLOSSARY

breed
To come together to have babies.

hover
To stay flying in the air in one spot.

marshes
Grassy wetlands that are similar to swamps.

migrate
To move from one part of the world to another.

predators
Animals that hunt and eat other animals.

prey
An animal that is hunted and eaten by another animal.

rodents
Small, furry animals with large front teeth, such as rats or mice.

stiff
Not easy to bend.

TO LEARN MORE

BOOKS

Hamilton, S. L. *Hawks*. Minneapolis: Abdo Publishing, 2018.

Huddleston, Emma. *How Birds Fly*. Minneapolis: Abdo Publishing, 2021.

Sommer, Nathan. *Hawks*. Minneapolis: Bellwether Media, 2019.

ONLINE RESOURCES

Visit **www.apexeditions.com** to find links and resources related to this title.

ABOUT THE AUTHOR

Connor Stratton writes and edits nonfiction children's books. He loves observing birds wherever he goes.

INDEX

Answer Key:
1. Answers will vary; **2.** Answers will vary; **3.** A; **4.** B; **5.** B; **6.** C